Classroom Quotes

Copyright © 2017 by Mike Artell

All rights reserved. This book or any portion thereof may not be reproduced or used in any manner whatsoever without the express written permission of the publisher except for the use of brief quotations in a book review.

Printed in the United States of America
ISBN 978-0-9910894-8-2

MJA Creative, LLC
Box 3997 Covington, LA   70434

All clip art used in this book is in the public domain courtesy of clker.com except for the drawing on Page 67 which was created by Mike Artell.

A boy in my class proudly announced that his mother had had a baby girl the previous night. "How much did she weigh?" I asked. "Six pounds and one **ouch**," he replied.

The kindergarten students were asked if they would like to say anything to our retiring school principal. One little girl stood up and said, "I hope you get a new job."

It was a Friday but I was determined to find that spring in my step so I donned my cute jean skirt and sneakers. As I waltzed into my third-grade classroom one of the boys said, "Mrs. F., you look like an old teacher tryin' to be young."

I asked one of my students to point to his elbow. He looked all over his entire body and then said, "I know I have one. I just don't know where it is."

During Fire Prevention week, some firefighters visited our class. One of them asked if any of my first-graders knew what a walkie-talkie was used for. One of my students shouted out, "To call for back up!"

I got a pet update from one of my students:

"You know my dogs Petey and Andy? Well, Andy has a girlfriend but Petey doesn't because they took his baby-makin' stuff and now he doesn't even WANT to get married."

It was a sad day when one of my students announced that her grandmother had died of ammonia.

On show-and-tell day one of the little girls in my class was excited to show her new pom-poms to her classmates.

She proudly marched to the front of the room, held them up for all her classmates to see and said, "These are tampons."

I teach first grade and occasionally my 80-year-old father will visit the classroom. The children lovingly call him Grandpa K. One morning when my father was visiting, one of my students was overcome with curiosity. He rose up out of his seat, crossed the room, and looked up at my dad and asked, "Grandpa K, how are you still alive?"

One of my students was a bit slow finishing his paper reindeer. When I announced that it was time to clean up, he looked up with a worried face and said, "Wait! Mine doesn't have any of those…those…anteaters on top."

The children in my class had become very noisy so I sat down, stopped talking and folded my hands in my lap. When they quieted down, I asked them if they knew why I had been waiting. One little boy suggested, "You were waiting until you finished your prayers."

My student explained, "I couldn't read my homework book last night because my dad was too busy stalking you on Facebook."

I was speechless!

I like to play with the kids during calendar time pretending that I don't know how to spell a month or a day of the week. One day as I was doing this, one of my students leaned over to another child and said, "I thought she would know this stuff by now."

One of my girls was sitting on the carpet squirming and pulling at her clothes. When I asked what she was doing, she replied, "I'm having a bad panty day!"

I ran into one of my students and his mother at the supermarket. He looked at me with shock and asked, "Who's watching the school?"

I have a small refrigerator in my room in which I keep a little food for the homemaking center and a few personal items. One day, one of my students was getting something from the refrigerator for me and after opening the door he turned and shouted to the rest of the class, "She LIVES here!"

We were doing a unit on money. One of my students came up to me and said, "Look. My two quarters were born the same year."

As one of my Kinder student's moms was writing a note to me, the child said, "Mom... you're going to have to change that because my teacher can't read cursive. That's why she teaches kindergarten."

While working individually with a little boy, I asked him what kind of work his dad did.

He gave me a detailed answer of his dad's profession and then looked at me and asked, "What kind of work do you do?"

I came outside to pick up my students from recess. One of my students said, "Mrs. S, have you lost your voice? Usually there is so much coming out of your mouth and there wasn't when you came outside."

One day in class we talked about different jobs people have. Kaylee was pretty excited to tell us where her mother worked. So I asked her, "Where does she work?". She said with a big grin "She works at the whore house". My mouth dropped. She explained, "You know... the big building in the middle of the square." I said, "You mean the COURT House?" She smiled and said, "Yeah, that's the place."

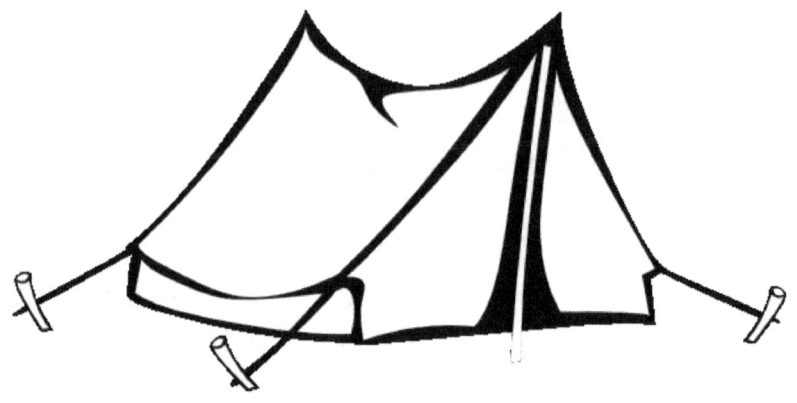

My second graders were learning about writing lists. One of my boys said he made a list of stuff to take camping, so I asked him to tell me one thing he was taking. He said, "Protection."

I just about died!

We were studying the planets and one of my students was looking at the planet "Uranus" and really admiring it. He said to me "Man Miss K, Uranus is so smooth! There are hardly any cracks or bumps!" It took everything I had not to crack up laughing.

We had been working with the children to use their words when they needed something from another child. A child who is normally well behaved hit another child.

When he was told to use his words when he wanted something, he answered," I DID use my words; he wouldn't listen."

My student walked up to me and said, "You look old!" I explained that's not a very nice thing to say to someone to which he replied, "I know you're not REALLY old. You just LOOK old!"

Last year I was talking with one of my kindergarteners about how we behave on the carpet. I was asking him what I could do to help him keep his body in his square. His reply was, "You will need to get some rope and tie me in it."

One morning I announced the lunch choices for the day. #1 was chicken patty and #2 was Salisbury steak. All the children signed up for lunch and we went about our day.

As we went through the lunch line, one of my students expressed his disappointment. "Oh, I thought you said STRAWBERRY steak."

A girl in my class was telling me about her middle school sister.

"My sister has a boyfriend. He is the "ex" kind of boyfriend. Have you ever heard of that kind of boyfriend?"

One of the young boys in my class was having trouble working with the wooden blocks. He threw the blocks on the floor and shouted an expletive. The boy sitting next to him said, "You shouldn't say that. It's a cursive word."

One of my students told his Dad that they have big journals at school. His dad was impressed. "Wow! You write in journals at school?" "No," his son said. "We pee in them." (urinals)

We took my third graders on a field trip to the Mark Twain Cave in Missouri. One of the areas was a tight fit. A little boy turned to me and said, "I can't go through tight places because I get constipated." He meant to say that he was claustrophobic.

A little girl who was very quiet told me about a pancake fight that occurred at her house that morning. I said I bet that was fun. She replied, "Not really. My mom was mad at my dad and she threw pancakes at him all the way to the bathroom."

A student had been getting "Oops notes" (unacceptable behavior notes). When he came to school I asked him what his mom said when she saw the notes and he replied, "Mrs. V those notes just keep flying out that bus window!"

I allow my students to enter the classroom as soon as they arrive at school. Before the bell rings, they can go to the bathroom or get a drink freely, they just need to let me know they are going. One morning a young man said, "'I'm going to the b--you know, bathroom." I said, "Okay, got you!" Not to be outdone, a little girl said, "I'm going to the j." I said, "What? What's the j?" She said, "You know the jurrr---ink." (drink!)

We'd been instructed to give students a reminder that shirt straps had to be at least two fingers wide. If they came to school with spaghetti straps showing, they'd have to change.

The next day a little girl came to school and walked straight to the bathroom. When I followed her and asked her what was wrong, she sadly replied, "I'm going to have to change my clothes. I'm wearing pizza straps."

A boy in my school looks just like his father and one morning I asked him, "Has any one ever told you that you look just like your daddy?" The boy (who is in Kindergarten) replied "Yes, that's because we both have hairy backs and chests!"

We were sharing during Circle Time and one little girl shared this: "My mommy said she wishes my daddy would go get lost in the woods."

I explained to one of my preschoolers that nose-picking was rude. With his finger still in his nose he begged, "Please let me be rude just one more minute!"

Sometimes nursery rhymes get changed a little in early childhood classes. Two examples:

Jack fell down and broke his crayon...

The sheep's in the middle, the cow's in the corner...

A boy in my class was excited that his dog had had puppies. "Are they boy or girl puppies?" I asked. "We don't know," he replied. "They ain't got their eyes open yet."

I began to lose my voice due to a cold. "Mrs. J," one of my students suggested, "you need to change the batteries in your throat!"

"What do you call little girl horses?" I asked.

"Fillies!" a little girl in my class shouted proudly.

"And what do you call little boy horses?" I asked.

There was a moment of hesitation and then she shouted, "Phillips!"

The children each opened their lunches to see what the grownups had prepared for them. Cameron said excitedly, "Tomato ships! I LOVE tomato ships!" And he proudly held up his bag of potato chips.

Is today tomorrow?" Heather asked. "No," I explained. "Today is today. Why do you ask?"

"Yesterday you said we were going to paint tomorrow and I was wondering if tomorrow is today."

"Yes, Heather," I smiled. "Today is tomorrow if I said it yesterday."

Just before recess, the rain began to fall. One of the girls lamented, "Oh great. It's raining. That means we'll be pooped-up inside all day."

To help celebrate Chinese New Year, our class ate a Chinese meal. The fortune cookies had a fortune on one side and a lottery number on the other. One of my students turned to the other and said, "I don't know what this side says, but on the other side I got a phone number to call when I get home."

At the beginning of each school year, I explain to the students that the thing on the side of my nose is a mole and not a bug. After reading, "Miss Nelson Is Missing" to my class, I was pleased when several of my students deduced that Viola Swamp and Miss Nelson where the same person.

One of the girls in my class raised her hand and said, "YOU could never fool us like that. We would always know you by that big, black thing on your nose."

Physically, I could best be described as, "petite" so I was taken aback when one of my students who had obviously learned a new word attempted to compliment me by saying:

"Ms. A...you look voluptuous today."

We had just finished discussing parts of the body when I overheard a discussion in one of the centers. A child was explaining that, "Boys have peanuts, but girls don't."

The children had been outside writing on the sidewalk with chalk. One of my students came running up to me and announced, "Teacher! Teacher! I wrote something!" I hurried to take a look and I asked, "What did you write?" He looked confused and then said, "I don't know. I can't read yet."

We were discussing dinosaurs and the fact that they are no longer on the earth. One child jumped up and announced, "I know what happened! They died and now they stink!"

Our principal is starting to go bald on the top. One day a child asked, Ms. J, why does he get his hair cut with a hole in the middle?

A student said to our retiring superintendent: "Thanks for being such a Super Nintendo."

When a student complained of a tummy ache, I asked what she had eaten. "I just ate pudding, macaroni and fruit cottontail," she explained.

I asked one of my students why we use an apostrophe in the word, "won't." His answer: "Because it's a contraption."

One of my students who had been out for a couple of days came back to school and told me, "I'm not going to be abstinent today."

One of my students picked up a large shell I had brought to class. "Hey, listen!" she exclaimed. "It sounds just like they flushed the toilet."

One of my Pre-K kids fell and cut his head. As we were examining the wound, the child asked, "Can you see my meat?"

I asked my class what ship the Pilgrims travelled on to get to America. One student who was very anxious to answer waved his hand and shouted, "The Cauliflower!"

One of my students announced that he was going to walk home after school. I explained that his mom would not want him to walk home in this hard rain. "Yes, she would," he replied. "My coat has a lid on it."

While riding on a school bus during a field trip, I was talking with one of the 4-year-old girls in my class. After a few miles, she turned to me and said, "You're just a pretend teacher. You're really a mommy."

One of my students was walking in the hallway with her mom when they say our principal. "That's Mr. B," she explained to her mother. "I don't know what he does."

We were tasting various fruit as part of our food unit. One little boy picked up a small, red slice of fruit and asked, "May I have a bite of this pee-wee?"

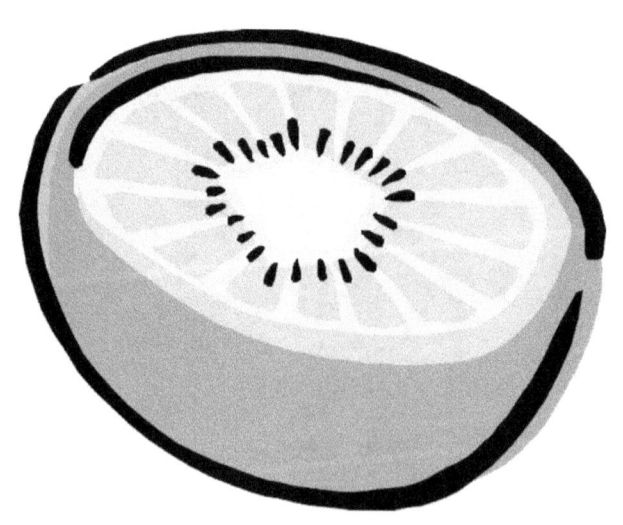

I became impatient with one of my students and told him I didn't like the way he was acting. "He looked at me and explained, "I'm not acting."

One of my students insisted that she felt, "NOSE-iated." When I asked her if she knew what that word meant, another child shouted from across the room, "Her NOSE hurts!"

I told my class that we would be making alphabet Jell-O jigglers. Later, one of the boys asked me when we would be making the gigolos.

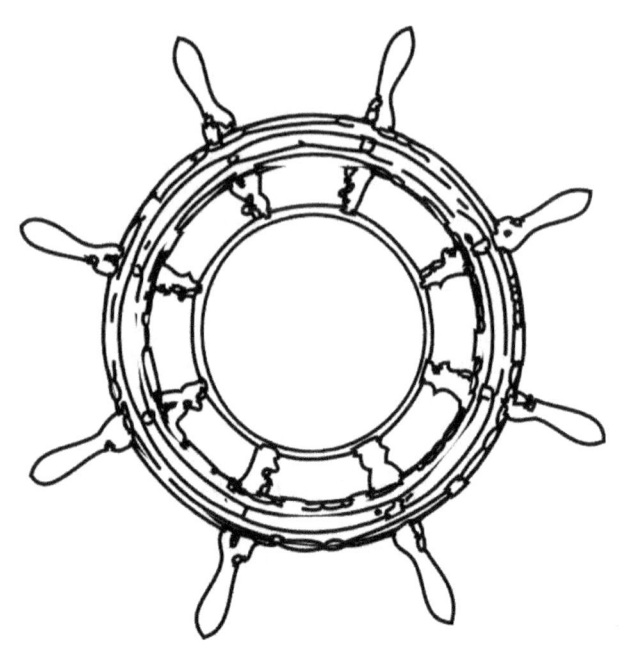

During October, I checked to see if my students remembered the names of Columbus's three ships. A very confident young man raised his hand and replied, "The Nina, the Santa Maria and the uh... Pinto Bean!"

One of the girls in my class raised her hand and asked, "Ms. M, may I go to the barf-room?"

At our small school, my students get to make spirit tags for the football team. One little boy raised his hand and asked me how to spell, "bitch." Naturally, I was a little shocked. I asked him how he was going to use it on the tag and he replied, "You know – like 2 bitch, 4 bitch, 6 bitch a dollar."

Our school is in a church building. One day, one of the children saw our pastor and proclaimed, "I know you. You're the man who yells at us every Sunday."

After listening to a partner's heartbeat in our class, one student said to her partner, "Girl… your heart sounds like a washing machine."

We were naming words that begin with the short "u" sound. I held up a picture and asked the children to name the man who stands behind the catcher at a baseball game. One boy raised his hand and shouted, "A vampire!"

We were doing some problem-solving games. I asked my class what they would do if they had 10 people coming for dinner and only 6 spoons. One of my clever girls said, "Send them all home."

One of my assertive little girls made her way to the front of the line and stated emphatically, "Pretty-K. I'm the lime leader!"

I reminded my students several times to bring money for the play we were going to attend. One day, one of my boys handed me four plastic chips and explained, "You've been telling us over and over to bring our PLAY money."

After I had everyone's attention I told them to remind their parents to bring them to the gym at 5:45 PM for our program. And I told them also that they should be dressed in Sunday attire. One boy gave me a confused look and asked, "We have to wear a TIRE?"

My student explained to me:

"This (E) is a capital E.

"This (e) is an uncapital E.

I asked one of my little girls which one of her toes was bothering her. She explained, "It's my thumbkin toe."

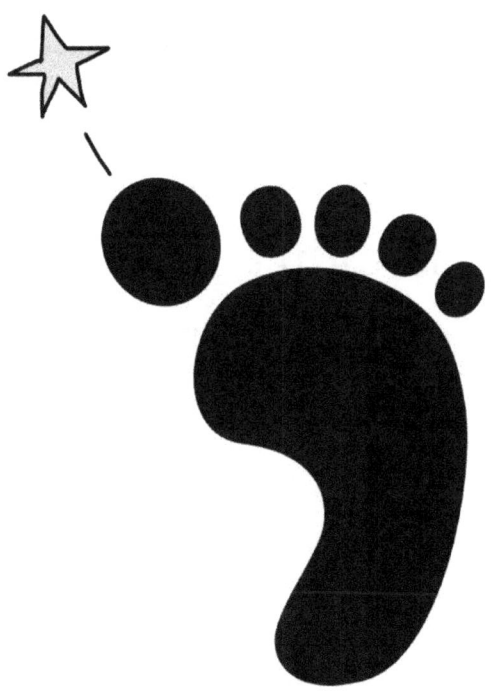

We were sharing our feelings about a tornado that recently touched down in our town. One of my students said, "My mama told me to get in the house. And that big tomato didn't get me."

One of the boys in my class spilled cherries and juice all over the floor. He began to clean up the mess and growled, "This is one weezun why dis school should have Stain Master carpets."

I was watching my students as they lined up for the water fountain. One of my students heard the school secretary paging me. She rushed down the hall and shouted, "Miss H. There's a message on your answering machine!"

After a very big hug, one of my little boys said, "You're going to go to heaven." Then after a pause, he added, "Because you're so old."

Our library media specialist was checking with me to be sure that students who had missed the state test would be given an opportunity to take it. "Do you have any make-ups?" she asked. One of the girls in my room looked up at me quizzically and asked, "She puts on your makeup?"

One of the little girls in my class had lost her sweater. I told her to go to the office and ask the principal if someone had turned it in. Later, the office secretary told me my student had asked for the, "princess."

A boy complained that glue would not flow from the bottle he was using. I suggested he turn it upside down and gravity would help.

The bewildered child looked up at me and asked, "Are you gravity?"

While administering a readiness test, a student asked me for the answer to one of the questions. "I can't give you the answer," I replied. The student then shot back, "Would you ask someone else the answer then?"

After I spent two and one-half hours in the beauty parlor the previous day, one of my little girls commented candidly, "Lord, Ms. T, you need to find yourself a new girl to do your hair!"

I spilled some water on my shoes and my socks and they were uncomfortably wet. One of my students suggested I could dry them in the bathroom. I thanked her for her suggestion but explained that I probably wouldn't have time between classes to do that. "O.K.," she said. "Good luck. Don't get a fungus."

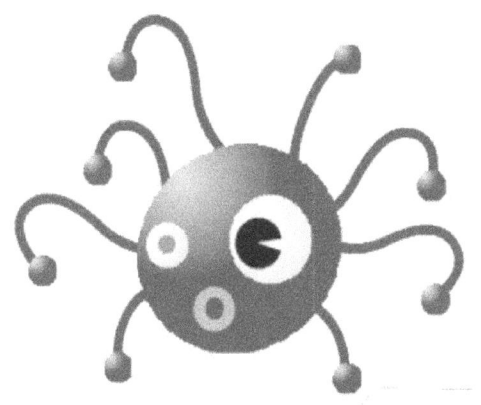

Good hygiene advice from one of my students:

"You should not put boogers on NOBODY!"

I asked my second-grade students what they think French people do on Thanksgiving since it is an exclusively American holiday. One of my girls said, "I think that's when they make French bread."

Can't argue with this logic from one of my students who found out his classmate had pink eye:

"Pink eye is better than a black eye."

One of my students explained, "I can't make a video of me reading with my grandma's phone. She has an old-fashioned phone — you know, the kind that only has numbers on it."

When we got to the part of the Pledge of Allegiance that says, "and to the republic, for which it stands...." one of my students turned to me and said, "I've been looking every day and I still can't find the WITCH that is supposed to be standing there!"

I was concerned about discussing the death of our classroom fish with my students. I didn't need to worry, however because one of my little boys offered this explanation to his classmates:

"I know what happened. It drank too much water."

And that was that.

I was in a different part of the school building when a 2nd grader saw me and asked where I was going. I told her I was heading back up to the library, to which she replied, "That's good. Because the library is nothing without you!"

Dear Mike Artell

I've been fortunate over the years to visit more than 1,000 schools in the U.S., Europe and Asia. Following my school visits, I often receive letters from kids with their personal notes. I've included copies of some of those letters on the following pages. Enjoy!

Mike Artell

Dear Mr. Artell,

Thank you for coming to our school and drawing with us. And thank you for making us miss math!

Sincerely,

Logan

Dear Mr. Artell,

I thought your drawings were much better then mine. When you read the book I almost peed my pants thats how hard I laughed.

                Nicole

Dear Mr. Artell,

I thought your drawings were much better than mine. When you read the book I almost peed my pants, that's how hard I laughed.

                Nicole

Dear Mike Artell,

I love your drawings! You must make a lot of money.

From,

Eliana

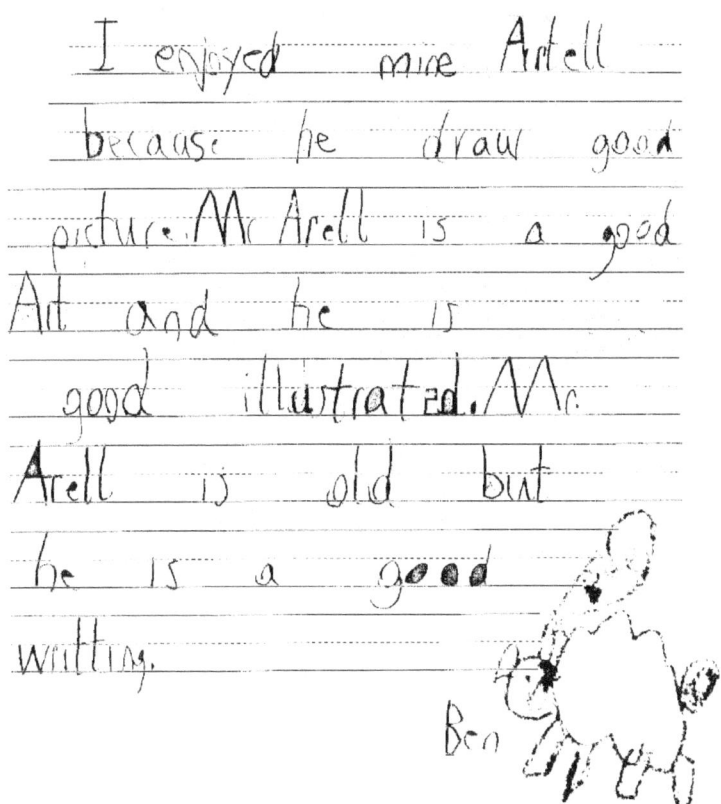

I enjoyed Mike Artell because he draws good pictures. Mr. Artell is a good artist and he is a good illustrator. Mr. Artell is old but he is a good writer.

Ben

> Dear Mike Artel
> I like your drawlings. Can you send me a letter. books are good and it's imponit to read because it makes you pass frist grod. this is my best hand withing.
>
> frome Katie

Dear Mike Artell:

I like your drawings. Can you send me a letter? Books are good and it's important to read because it makes you pass first grade. This is my best hand writing.

From Katie

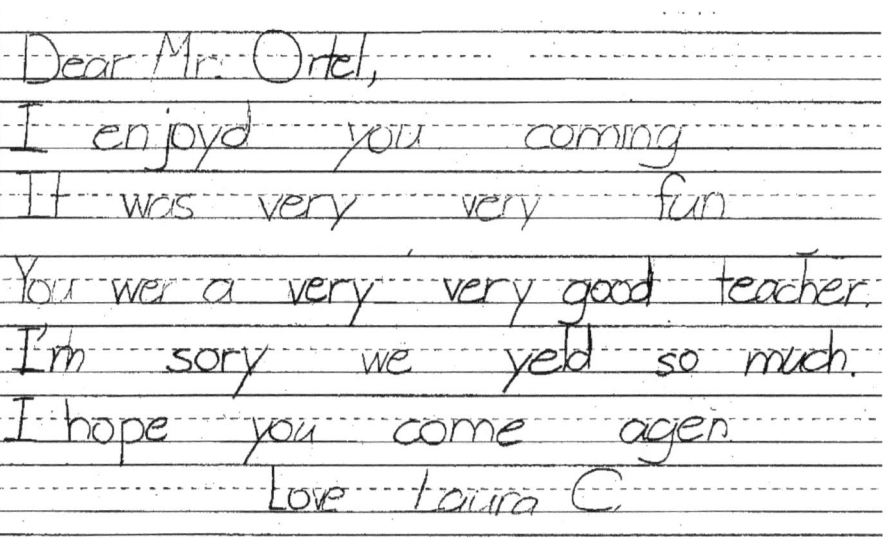

Dear Mr. Artell,

I enjoyed you coming. It was very, very fun. You were a very, very good teacher. I'm sorry we yelled so much. I hope you come again.

Love, Laura C.

Jonathan

I like you
I wish I kud bey yor
Sun

From Jonathan

I like you. I wish I could be your son.

Do you have a great Classroom Quote you'd like to share?

If you've got a memorable classroom quote you'd like to share, email it to Mike Artell at mike@mikeartell.com. Include the words, "classroom quotes" in the subject line.

Please be aware:

. All submissions must be something YOU have actually heard a child say.

. All quotes and associated rights to the quotes become the property of Mike Artell.

. There is no monetary compensation.

Mike Artell is a multi-award-winning children's book author, illustrator and musician. You can learn more about Mike's books and music by visiting his web site: www.mikeartell.com.

Mike also suggests that you do an Internet search on his name. You'll find lots of links with how-to-draw videos, music and interviews.

You can have Mike visit your school, speak at your conference or conduct a professional development workshop for your teachers. For complete information, email Mike at mike@mikeartell.com.

www.ingramcontent.com/pod-product-compliance
Lightning Source LLC
Chambersburg PA
CBHW070542300426
44113CB00011B/1763